LEGENDS AND MYTHS

# *TURTLE ISLAND STORIES*

WRITTEN BY
**RICHARD NANAWIN**

RICHARD NANAWIN

Turtle Island Stories

*Copyright © 2023 by Richard Nanawin*

*All rights reserved. No part of this publication may be reproduced, stored or transmitted in any form or by any means, electronic, mechanical, photocopying, recording, scanning, or otherwise without written permission from the publisher. It is illegal to copy this book, post it to a website, or distribute it by any other means without permission.*

*This novel is entirely a work of fiction. The names, characters and incidents portrayed in it are the work of the author's imagination. Any resemblance to actual persons, living or dead, events or localities is entirely coincidental.*

*Richard Nanawin asserts the moral right to be identified as the author of this work.*

*Richard Nanawin has no responsibility for the persistence or accuracy of URLs for external or third-party Internet Websites referred to in this publication and does not guarantee that any content on such Websites is, or will remain, accurate or appropriate.*

*Designations used by companies to distinguish their products are often claimed as trademarks. All brand names and product names used in this book and on its cover are trade names, service marks, trademarks and registered trademarks of their respective owners. The publishers and the book are not associated with any product or vendor mentioned in this book. None of the companies referenced within the book have endorsed the book.*

*First edition*

*ISBN: 978-1-7773352-3-6*

*Editing by Mr Pat Cuthbert*

*This book was professionally typeset on Reedsy. Find out more at reedsy.com*

*During my lifetime I have listened to and learned from many Indigenous Elders, Clan Mothers, and Hereditary Chiefs, this book is dedicated to those who inspired me along the way.*

*Basil Ambers*
*William George*
*Albert Wilson*
*Rupert Wilson,*
*William Edenshaw*
*Susan Abraham*
*William George*
*Larry Grant,*
*John Henderson*
*Beau Dick*

"Let us put our minds together and see what life we can make for our children"

Sitting Bill

# Contents

| | | |
|---|---|---:|
| *Preface* | | ii |
| *Acknowledgement* | | iii |
| 1 | Nanabush and the Great Buzzard | 1 |
| 2 | The White-Faced Bear | 4 |
| 3 | The Salmon Story | 11 |
| 4 | Wolf Clan and the Salmon | 14 |
| 5 | Why Buffalo has a Hump | 16 |
| 6 | Raven and the Origin of the Tide | 18 |
| 7 | The Wild Woman of the Woods (Dzonokwa) | 22 |
| 8 | How Rabbit Fooled Wolf | 25 |
| 9 | The Creation Story | 30 |
| 10 | When Tcikabis Trapped the Sun | 33 |
| 11 | How Deer Fawns got their Spots | 36 |
| 12 | Beaver Meat | 38 |
| 13 | Origin of Language | 40 |
| 14 | The Woman and the White Bear | 43 |
| 15 | The Legend of White Horse Plains | 47 |
| 16 | Raven fools Crow | 50 |
| 17 | The Pact of the First | 54 |
| 18 | The Story of Jumping Mouse | 56 |
| 19 | How Music came to the World | 66 |
| 20 | The Bully and the Buffalo | 70 |

# Preface

During my lifetime, I have traveled to, lived on, and visited many Turtle Island Nations; from the Kwakiutl Nation to the west, the Tahltan the far north, and the Micmac to the far east. When the opportunity arose, I would seek out Elders and Knowledge Keepers and listen to their stories with a child's delight. This collection of stories is dedicated to the many I met along the way, the ones who are no longer with us and those whose stories have not yet be heard.

*Richard Nanawin*

# Acknowledgement

*"I have to start by thanking my awesome wife, Sherri. From reading early drafts to giving me advice on the cover to keeping the Teens out of my hair so I could edit, she was as important to this book getting done as I was. Thank you so much, dear."*

# 1

# Nanabush and the Great Buzzard

*An Ojibwa Story*

Many years ago, the great Buzzard was flying highin the air; he looked down and saw Nanabush wandering across the middle of the meadow. So the great Buzzard decided to visit with Nanabush; he pointed his beak towards the earth, spread his great wings and soared close to the ground. When the great Buzzard was close to the ground, Nanabush spoke to him, "Great Buzzard, you must see everything happening on the earth while you are flying in the sky; please take on your back so I can see what you see when soaring over the land, please take me to your world.

The Great Buzzard swooped down and landed beside Nanabush; he was a tall creature with beautiful feathers and wings with long feathers."Climb upon my back Nanabush, hold on tight; I will take you to my world high in the sky"; Nanabush climbed upon the back of the Great Buzzard; he said, "Your feathers are very smooth; I may slip off. Please do not turn suddenly, or I may fall off." The Great Buzzard said, "I will be careful, hang on tight." However, the Great Buzzard had no intention of keeping his promise. With a great leap and a forceful run, the Great Buzzard spread his wings and took to the air. As they flew, Nanabush held on as the Great Buzzard's body twisted while he soared towards the sun high in the sky.

Nanabush was amazed by what he saw; many trees and mountains looked smaller and smaller as they flew high above the earth; he saw the marshland, lakes and streams like never before. Suddenly, the Great Buzzard swooped upward and turned over, Nanabush tried to hang on, but he lost his grip and fell to earth like a stone. Nanabush hit the muddy ground near a marsh; the cruel landing knocked him senseless; As he came too and stood up, he could see the Great Buzzard soaring in circles high above, laughing at him. Nanabush said, "You have tricked me, Great Buzzard, but I will get my revenge someday; you'd better watch out." The Great Buzzard flew closer and said, "Nanabush, you may try, but you will not trick me; I'll always be looking for you."

Nanabush waited until the Great Buzzard flew away out of sight. Then, he sat down to plan his revenge; he thought and thought until he realized Great Buzzard only eats dead animals. Nanabush went to the edge of the mountain meadow; he transformed himself into a dead deer. He knew the Great Buzzard could not resist fresh dead meat. So, Nanabush was out in the open meadow so the Great Buzzard could spot him from high in the sky. After a short time, many other scavengers, beasts, and bugs began to gorge themselves on the dead deer carcass. The Great Buzzard soaring above noticed the activity below; he thought, "That Nanabush is up to something; he's trying to trick me."

The Great Buzzard swooped over the dead deer several times to have a good look; he finally decided to join the other scavengers and feast for himself on fresh dead meat. When he landed and approached the dead deer, he thought, "It's truly a dead deer; Nanabush can't fool me." So the Great Buzzard dug his beak deep inside the deer. He grabbed hold of the intestines and fat without realizing his entire head was inside the deer carcass. Suddenly the dead sprang to life, closing the wounded flesh around the Great Buzzard's neck and trapping him inside.

Nanabush said, "See, I could trick you after all; now pull your head from my flesh." As the Great Buzzard pulled his head from the flesh, he could feel burning pain; he knew he was losing feathers.

When his head finally emerged, all the feathers on his head and neck were gone; all left was bumpy red skin down his neck. For his deceit and trickery that hurt Nanabush, the Great Buzzard forever lost his beautiful head feathers and remains featherless to this day.

# 2

# The White-Faced Bear

*An Aleut Story*

A long time ago, there was a great Bear hunter in the Northlands. He was always successful, and he never failed to return home to his village without a Bear. Many other hunters were proud of his skills but tried to convince him to stop hunting so much. One hunter said, "Take what you need, but if you keep killing Bears, someday a great beast may just kill you." The great hunter said, "I'll take what I want and kill every Bear that crosses my path." A few weeks later, in the early summer season, the great hunter was out on the barrens; he spotted a mother and two cubs; he said, "She's not too big; this will be easy." Using his bow, he killed the mother Bear; the cubs ran away across the barren lands, not to be seen again.

The Great Bear hunter returned home to his village once more with the mother Bear on his sled; the other local hunter said, "We only take what we need; please stop killing mother Bears." About a month later, the great Bear hunter was out on the barrens, he had not seen any Bears, but he met a man from another village. He did not know who he was. The man said there were many Bears around his town, but a mighty white Bear killed many village hunters.

The man said hunters watched the tremendous white Bear tear apart a man like he was searching for something; he would not eat the man; everyone knew him by his white head and white paws. The Great Bear hunter thanked the villager for his company and his information. He said, "I am not afraid to kill any Bear, even a man killing one."

The great hunter continued across the barrens and found a small creek. He searched for fish, but none were in the stream. The Great Bear hunter was hoping the Bear would be at the creeks searching for fish to eat, as it would make hunting easier. Finally, the great hunter settled down for the night under the stars. The northern lights were dancing across the night. An Elder had told him that the northern lights were the spirits of a walrus playing with the skull of an unfortunate walrus hunter. After the great Bear hunter had awoken, he made his way to the top of a great hill. He looked out on the barrens and saw many Bears in small groups of one or two.

While looking across the barrens, he spotted the feared white Bear in a tiny group. His head and paws were a brilliant white; the rest of him was dark brown. He was an impressive figure among the backdrop of other smaller Bears. The Great Bear hunter decided to wait for the great beast to be alone before he struck the final blow. Unknown to the great Bear hunter, the feared great white Bear was once a man just like him – an impressive great hunter who believed himself above others. Many other great hunters had been jealous and had made plans to end his selfish reign over them.

Some great hunters travelled across the barrens to the mountains to the south, looking for a Shaman. They wanted the Shaman to turn the man they disliked into the creature he so feverishly pursued. So the Shaman told the great hunters to seek out a Bear, kill it and bring to skin back.

While the Great Bear hunter was sleeping by his small fire, the Shaman walked silently over to the sleeping great Bear hunter and placed the dead-skinned Bear on the sleeping hunter. When the Great Bear hunter awoke the following day, he discovered he had been transformed into the beast he hunted so well. Looking down into the saw, his hands had been turned into great white paws. He got up, walked over to the nearby stream, and looked into the water. He saw a great Bear staring back at him with a glowing white face. Before the Shaman left, he told the other great hunters they would know the man when they saw the white face and paws. Then Shaman retreated into the barrens, never to be seen again.

The Great Bear hunter spent his day high on the hill, waiting for the small Bears to leave. Sometime later, he noticed the white-faced great was by himself with no others near him. The white-faced Bear began to move toward the hill. The Great Bear hunter moved closer to the ground so as not to be seen by the white-faced Bear. Just as he was about to lift his head, the shadow of the white-faced Bear was now blocking out the sunlight above him. "Why are you here!!?" boomed the voice of the white face Bear. The great hunter answered, "I am here to hunt you."

The white-faced great said, "You have killed many members of my family, you have killed my wife, and now you here to kill me. Had you killed my children, I would have killed you now and torn you apart. I will spare your life today if you promise not to hunt Bears anymore; many of the Bears you saw from here are my other children and my brothers; never hunt us again, or I will tear you into pieces".

The Great Bear hunter was grateful to be spared by the white-faced Bear; he gathered his bow and returned to his village. When he was near his town, he met another Bear hunter; he shared the story of his encounter with the white-faced great; the other Bear hunter told him, "You may hunt but never hunt Bear again." Some time passed before the great Bear hunter went hunting again; he eventually went out with six other Bear hunters; they headed for the same hill where the great Bear hunter had his encounter with the white-faced Bear. Once at the mountain, they saw many Bears foraging on the barrens below; the white-faced great was nowhere to be seen. So they followed the great Bear hunter down towards the Bear below when one of the other Bear hunters said, "I see the white-faced great over there."

The Great Bear hunters also saw the white-faced Bear and retreated to the other side of the hill to avoid the white-faced Bear. Once on the other side, they saw many Bears; they each used their bows and killed seven Bears; the great Bear hunter had also killed one himself. As the great hunters started the long journey back to their villages across the barrens, the great Bear hunter was at the back of the group. Then, suddenly, he could hear a noise behind him.

When he looked back, the white-faced Bear ran towards him; he took out his bow, placed an arrow, and shot toward the white-faced Bear. The arrow missed!!, the white-faced Bear stopped in front of him and said, "Why did you try to kill me ? I did not hurt you the last time we met". The Great Bear hunter found himself helpless on the ground; the white face Bear spoke again, "This great hunter killed my wife and many of my brothers and sisters; I told his man I would tear him apart piece by piece if he hunted Bears again. So you are free to go; you brought no harm to me today. The other six hunters ran away as fast as possible, leaving the great Bear hunter to suffer his fate.

The white face Bear spoke, "I spared your life once before when you promised never to hunt Bear again; you brought many more Bear hunters this time; I will do to you as you have done to my family." The Great Bear hunter pleaded with the white-faced Bear to let him return home one last time to say goodbye to his family; the white-faced Bear at first refused but eventually said, "I will give you your life back; in return, you must lead me to the man who transformed me." The Great Bear hunter said he had been told a Shaman from the southern mountains had transformed him into a beast. He agreed to lead the white-faced Bear to the Shaman the following evening.

The Great Bear hunter reached his village in the morning, and the six hunters were surprised to see him alive and well. He retold his conversation with the white-faced Bear and his promise to lead him to the Shaman who'd transformed him. The Great Bear hunter asked his companions to join him. They all refused and tried vainly to warn him not to return to the barrens. That night, the great Bear hunter met the white-faced Bear at the forest's edge. He led him to a small clearing where there was a small hide-covered hut, the home of the Shaman. The white-faced Bear spoke, "Go to the Shaman and bring him outside to speak with me." The Great Bear hunter went to the entrance; it was tied closed from the inside. He called out to the Shaman to come out to speak with him. The Shaman had been sleeping; he said, "Who is this person who dares come to my home"; the great Bear hunter said, "I have come to speak with you. Can you come outside? There is a man who wants to speak with you". The Shaman was very tired, but he got up, untied his entrance, and exited into the moonlight; he was unaware that he was walking into a trap.

When the Shaman got his eyes to focus, he was standing before the white-faced Bear he had transformed many years ago; the white-faced Bear spoke," You are the one responsible for the torture I have endured these past years, I ask you now to transform me back to the man I was, or I will tear you to pieces." The Shaman promised he would do his best to end his suffering, the white-faced Bear and the Shaman re-entered the hut, and the work began. Many hours passed, and the Great Bear hunter waited patiently outside; he could hear screams and howls of pain coming from inside the Shaman's hut.

They both emerged from the hut the following day; the white-faced Bear was now back to his form as a man; he was carrying the great skin that had burdened him so long. The Shaman asked the man if he could have this great skin; the man cut off the head and paws and gave the rest back to the Shaman. The man spoke to the Shaman, "Do not ever transform anyone in the Bear again; if you do, I will return and kill you dead." The man and the great Bear hunter left the Shaman's hut and walked toward the barrens; the man spoke, "Do not ever hunt Bear again; you may hear others say they have seen me, do not join the hunt; if you do, I will kill you dead."

Many months later, the great hunter was at home and keeping his promise not to hunt Bears when two young men came to his village looking for him. They had spotted the white-faced Bear and wanted him to help them track it down. The great hunter thought for a while and then decided to help the young men; he would disguise himself and not carry a bow to hunt. So the great Bear hunter gathered all the Bear hunters together, and they all headed out to hunt down and kill the white-faced great once and for all.

As the group arrived at the hill, the white-faced Bear rose from the ground, shook himself in anger, and roared; the Chief Bear hunter called out and said, "We must stand and fight. He is too dangerous to leave alive". Then, with a great huff and roar, the white-faced Bear ran towards the group of great hunters; he found the disguised great hunter first, tore him to pieces, dug a shallow hole, and buried him.

The remaining Bear hunters tried to escape, but the white-faced Bear chased them down, tore them all to pieces, and buried them. Then, the white-faced Bear returned to the home of the Shaman and pulled him to pieces and buried him in a shallow hole in front of this hut.

The white-faced Bear returned to the barrens and rested, never to be seen again by man's eyes.

# 3

# The Salmon Story

*A Haida Story*

Many years ago, the daughter of a great Chief was crying; she cried and cried for something that no one could give her; none of the other Chiefs or the Old wise men could give the gift she desperately wanted, a great gleaming, leaping shiny fish. Her father sought out the oldest elder and asked if the fish did exist. The elder said they had never seen a shiny fish that size near their home inlets. As the days turned into weeks, his daughter's persistent sadness and crying made her sick; the great Chief decided to call upon the Counsel to address his daughter's suffering.

The Chief called upon all the Elders and Shaman to meet around the fire the next day; one of the wise Elders spoke, "The girl cries for a fish she has seen in her dreams, we have a lot of big fish in our inlets, but none are the kind your daughter cries for. If such a fish exists, it would be valuable to our community if we could find it and let all who have attended speak. Maybe one of us will know where the gleaming leaping fish can be found".

One elderly shaman stood and acknowledged the Chief; he then spoke, "Our friend the Raven lives in the great cedars. He is wise and knows many things we do not; I would like him to come to our Counsel fire to offer his knowledge." The Chief asked the elderly shaman to seek out the Raven. The elderly shaman left and returned quickly with a Raven perched on his shoulder. The Raven spoke in a raspy tone, "Your daughter cries for the great Salmon in her dreams. During this season, they are found near the mouth of a mighty river far from here. I will help stop your daughter's cries. I will fly as fast as possible and bring back one of the great, gleaming leaping fish she seeks.

The Chief rose to thank the Raven, but he'd flown out the door before he could thank him for his offer to help his daughter. The Raven flew high and far, his keen eyes keeping an eye out for Salmon near the river mouth. He saw a great many near the mouth of the mighty river. The Raven tucked his wings back and dove towards the water, his eyes sharp and his claws out, ready to grab the Salmon. Instead, the Raven swooped over the water, reached down and captured a Salmon in his talons, and flew back towards the sky.

The Raven did not realize he'd captured the son of Salmon Chief. The Salmon Scouts leap from the water, looking for the direction the Raven had flown away. The Salmon Chief and many Salmon followed, leaping in great arcs from the water as they followed the Raven flying over the water. The Salmon Chief chased the Raven as fast as possible, but the Raven was far ahead. The Raven flew in circles before seeing the Chief's Daughter. He landed beside her and laid the fish at her feet; she smiled and cried no more.

The Raven spoke to the Chief in a raspy tone," The Salmon Chief has followed me with many of his kind; he will indeed enter the inlet to rescue his son that I have brought here."

The Chief said," Tie your nets into a giant woven net. When the Salmon enter our inlet, we will trap them." The villagers worked fast to prepare the catch. The Salmon entered the inlet just as the Raven said. The villagers strung the net across and captured all the Salmon. To keep them, prisoner, the long leather thong was passed through the gills of each Salmon; one end was tied to a giant boulder in the inlet, the other to the base of a great Totem in front of the Chief's house. The pole began to grow as high as a giant cedar. A Thunderbird was carved on the top, followed by a Chief, an Raven and a Salmon; this Totem is called 'nhe-is-bik,' the tethering pole. Since this time, generations of Salmon have followed the same route to the inlet during the springtime; the people are thankful for Raven's gift.

# 4

# Wolf Clan and the Salmon

*A Tsimshian Legend*

Many years ago, a large clan lived along the Nass River. Each year, they would gather at the headwaters, where they had access to abundant Salmon and wild berries. Each year's abundance made the village well respected and prosperous for generations. However, as the generations came and went, young men began to ignore the traditional ways of doing things. Over time, some young men started killing animals and leaving them out for the eagles and crows. When the Salmon season was upon them, some young men from the village would catch many Salmon, cut a slit in their backs and place burning pine pitch in the wound. Then, the young men would release the Salmon back into the River. They swam away in terror with their backs ablaze like living torches.

The young men thought nothing of the wastefulness or pain they inflicted upon the Salmon. The Elders tried as they might, but the young men would not take their advice. The Chief of the Sky would become angered at their behaviour. As time passed, the hon season was once again coming. The clans would soon be preparing for the winter season's ceremonial feasts. While the clans worked to retrieve the Salmon, they could hear a strange noise in the distance; it sounded like great drums being struck repeatedly. The clan old people knew the noise was a warning sign of bad things coming to everyone.

How the Young men treated, the Salmon had angered the Chief of the Sky. So although the Clan Elders once again warned the young men not to harm them, they ignored the Elder words.

While the Clan continued to collect, dry and store their Salmon, the sound of the great drum grew louder and closer; this worried the young men. The Elders would blame them should harm come to the people. Then, a few days later, a distant mountain exploded with a thunderous explosion.

Fire and rock flowed into the Salmon rivers and the nearby forests. Very few Clan members escaped the mountain's fury. Later, Shamen would stay the Chief of the Sky and be angered by the disrespect shown towards the Salmon. He punished all those who harmed the creatures of Turtle Island for pleasure. However, the harm would not befall future Clans; they respected all creatures as gifts from the Chief of the Sky.

# 5

# Why Buffalo has a Hump

A Chippewa Legend

Many generations ago, when Turtle Island was young, the Buffalo that wandered the prairies had no hump. Eventually, the Buffalo would have a hump because he was foolish and caused harm to the feathered birds. When the Buffalo ran across the prairie, the Fox would run ahead to warn the other animals the Buffalo was coming. On one summer season day, the Buffalo was running across the prairie. He ran right towards where many feathered birds had their nests in the tall prairie grass. The feathered birds yelled to the Fox and the Buffalo to stop running. Their nests were on the ground in their path.

The Foxes jumped over the feathered bird nests, but the Buffalo ignored the feathered birds yelling; he forged ahead and trampled over the nests in the tall grass, his heavy hoofs destroying many nests. The feathered birds cried out loudly. Unknown to animals, Nanabush was nearby. He heard the feathered birds crying out. He saw the Fox and Buffalo running through the tall prairie grass. Nanabush felt sorry for the feathered birds. He ran across the prairie and grabbed a large fallen willow branch. He stood the path of charging Buffalo and struck him hard between the shoulders. The Buffalo stopped in his tracks. Knowing he'd angered Nanabush, he shrugged his shoulders one more time, expecting to be hit again.

However, Nanabush did not strike again; he said, "From this day forth, you shall have humped shoulders; your head will always hang in shame for the harm you caused the feathered birds." While the Buffalo was being punished, the Fox had run away and quickly dug holes in the prairie ground to hide; Nanabush saw them; he said, "Because you harmed the feathered bird, you will always live below the tall grass underground where it's cold."

Since that time, many generations ago, the Buffalo has always had a hump, and the foxes have lived underground.

# 6

# Raven and the Origin of the Tide

*A Tlingit Legend*

Many years ago, Turtle Island was new, and there existed Raven people. They all lived new the great water. During this time, there were no tide waters; the Raven people would gather their food from the great water and eat all things that washed up on shore, especially clams. However, as time passed, the abundance of the clams was ebbing away, the water was too deep, and the Raven people could not gather enough food to feed themselves. As a result, ravens were often greedy and would eat all things washed up on shore, leaving nothing for anyone else.

Raven was always hungry; he always wanted his belly full of clams; he began to think about how to solve this belly problem. As he sat, he began to think; he eventually fell into a deep dream sleep. While he was dreaming, he was visited by the Great Spirit: who said,

"Dear Raven, I have seen your hunger, and I pity you and your people who feed on the great water. You must search the edge of the great water and look for a cave. In the cave, you shall find an old woman. The woman in the cave holds the tide line on her lap. She is powerful, so you must trick her into releasing the tide line from her grip. The great water will recede when she releases the tide line, and an abundance of clams and other food will become visible. You are a clever creature, so that I will leave the trickery up to your imagination".

When Raven woke up, he could feel the hunger in his belly. He knew he had to follow the advice given to him by the great spirit. So Raven took off high into the moon and flew for many days. Raven only takes a few hours each day to rest his tired wings along the way. Eventually, he reached the edge of the great water. When Raven approached the edge of the great water, he saw a cave in the distance. He landed near the entrance and peered inside. The great spirit was correct; the old woman was sitting in the back of the cave with the tide line on her lap, gripped by her hands. Raven knew he must trick the old woman into releasing the tide line. He stood at the cave entrance and said: "My belly is full; what a great clam feast I have discovered!!".

Suddenly the old woman spoke, "Raven, Raven, where did you get those clams ?; Raven continued," There's another clam and another; my belly will surely be full soon!!"

The old woman leaned forward; she tried to see what Raven was eating, "Raven, where did you get all those clams ?; Raven ignored the old woman and talked about his bounty of clams. Finally, Raven said: "Those were tasty; I'm going to take some home." The old woman leaned forward even more; her neck stretched as far as it could to see what Raven was doing. The Raven kicked up sand into the old woman's eyes. She released the tide line from her grip and rubbed her eyes to get the sand out. When the old woman released the tide line, the water began to recede; Raven was happy and flew home to enjoy his new bounty of food. When the Raven arrived home, the great water had receded, his people enjoyed their new bounty, gorged themselves each day for many weeks, and their bellies were full.

As time passed, Raven noticed many of the great water creatures were dying and washed up on the shallow shore, their bodies rotting on the rocks. Raven soon realized that the great water had receded too far; the great water creatures they depended on for food were dying. They would surely perish if he did not make the water rise again.

Raven took to the sky again; he flew for many days, resting very little as he headed for the old woman's cave. When Raven arrived at the old woman's cave, she was still trying to get the sand out of her eyes; she said," Raven, have you come back to trick me again!! help me get the sand out of my eyes and find the tide line I have dropped". Raven said, "Yes, old woman, my trickery worked on you; the great water receded after you released the tide line. My people ate many good things from under the great water, and their bellies were full; the great water creatures began to die, their bodies smelled, and they washed up on our shallow shore. So if you help my people, release the tide line each day for a short time, I will help you get the sand out of your eyes". The old woman said, "Very well, I will release the tide line each day as the moon passes, this will help your people and the great creatures of the great water."

Raven helped the old woman get the sand out of her eyes and found the tide line she had dropped; the water began to rise again once it was in her firm grip. Raven left and flew home, just as promised. The great water would recede when the moon rose and fell. This pleased Raven and all the great water creatures.

# RAVEN AND THE ORIGIN OF THE TIDE

# 7

# The Wild Woman of the Woods (Dzonokwa)

*A Kwakiutl Legend*

The Wild Woman of the woods was a forest dweller. She was known by many names by the Kwakiutl people of northwest Vancouver Island. This story was told to me by Hereditary Chief Basil Amber at his cabin in Tsakis many years ago; I am honoured to retell his story.

Dzonokwa would appear at potlatches, dance around the fire in the wrong direction, and often annoy other dancers. She would move slowly, eventually falling and going to sleep. Attendants would then pick her up and take her to a seat where she would fall asleep again. When she arose again, she would transform to male form and oversee giving the Chief's possessions away.

Many seasons ago, Elders would share the story of Dzonokwa with the village's children; they warned the children not to venture into the forest after dark, or Dzonokwa might capture them. The villagers knew that when the sun was setting,

## THE WILD WOMAN OF THE WOODS (DZONOKWA)

Dzonokwa was hungry and near the village. They could hear her haunting screams, "OUGHHHH!!!OUGHHHH!.

Dzonokwa was easy to recognize; she had a pouty expression, and her bright red lips protruded from her face. Her hair was bushy and unkempt, and her eyes appeared half-closed and lay deep in her eye sockets. She had a gaunt skull-like face with pendulous breasts that hung to the ground. She was often seen walking in a shuffle, hunched over, carrying a woven basket over her shoulder. A little girl once lived on the ocean's edge in a coastal village. She was exceedingly small and referred to as the runt of the litter, last born and often teased by the village's other children.

The Elders had told her and all the other children to stay close to shore and not venture into the forest after dark. The hair ogress would capture them. One evening the children were playing too close to the forest edge; the sun was low in the sky. Suddenly, Dzonokwa leapt from behind a great cedar; she scooped up the children and put them all in her woven basket; she began the journey back to her mountain cave, where she would eat the children for dinner. The children struggled to free themselves, but to no avail; the woven basket lid was too tight to lift. The children saw daylight through a small hole in the bottom of the basket; they tore at weaving but could only make the hole a little bigger.

All the children tried to fit through the hole, but the only one that could do through was the sister that everyone had always teased. She took her turn, slipped quickly through the hole, and fell to the ground below. She ran back to the village to tell the Elders what had happened.

The Elders from the village quickly followed the trail left by Dzonokwa and found her cave; she had prepared a fire and was getting ready to eat the children in her basket. The Elders began to sing a song that made Dzonokwa tired; they watched as the great ogress stumbled toward the fire, tripping over her basket that released the children. The great ogress fell into the fire and burned to ember and ash. A great wind suddenly came up and blew the embers into the sky; these embers turned into thousands of mosquitos. To this day, children never question their Elder's advice, and Dzonokwa is still the form of the blood-searching mosquito with us.

# 8

# How Rabbit Fooled Wolf

A Native American Story

Two pretty girls lived not far from Rabbit and Wolf. So one day, Rabbit called upon Wolf and said, "Let's go and visit those pretty girls up the road."

"All right," Wolf said, and they started.

When they got to the girls' house, they were invited in, but both girls took a great liking to Wolf and paid all their attention to him while Rabbit had to sit by and look on. Rabbit, of course, was not pleased by this, and he soon said, "We had better be going back."

"Let's wait a while longer," Wolf replied, and they remained until late in the day. Before they left, Rabbit found a chance to speak to one of the girls so that Wolf could not overhear, and he said, "The one you've been having so much fun with is my old horse."

"I think you are lying," the girl replied.

"No, I am not. You shall see me ride him up here tomorrow."

"If we see you ride him up here," the girl said with a laugh, "we'll believe he's only your old horse."

When the two left the house, the girls said, "Well, call again."

The following day Wolf was up early, knocking on Rabbit's door. "It's time to revisit those girls," he announced.

Rabbit groaned. "Oh, I was sick all night," he answered, "and I hardly feel able to go."

Wolf kept urging him, and finally, Rabbit said, "If you let me ride you, I might go along to keep you company."

Wolf agreed to carry him astride his back. But then Rabbit said, "I would like to put a saddle on you to brace myself" When Wolf agreed to this, Rabbit added: "I believe it would be better if I should also bridle you."

Although Wolf objected at first to being bridled, he gave in when Rabbit said he did not think he could hold on and manage to get as far as the girls' house without a bridle. Finally, Rabbit wanted to put on the spurs.

"I am too ticklish," Wolf protested.

"I will not spur you with them," Rabbit promised. "I will hold them away from you, but it would be nicer to have them on."

At last, Wolf agreed to this, but he repeated: "I am very ticklish. You must not spur me."

"When we get near the girls' house," Rabbit said, "we will take everything off you and walk the rest of the way."

And so they started up the road, Rabbit proudly riding upon Wolf's back. Then, when they were nearly in sight of the house, Rabbit raked his spurs into Wolf's sides, and Wolf galloped full speed right by the house.

"Those girls have seen you now," Rabbit said. "I will tie you here and go up to see them and try to explain everything. Then, I'll come back after a while and get you."

And so Rabbit went back to the house and said to the girls:

"You both saw me riding my old horse, did you not?"

"Yes," they answered, and he sat down and had a good time with them.

After a while, Rabbit thought he ought to untie Wolf and started back to where he was fastened. He knew that Wolf must be very angry with him by this time, and he thought up a way to untie him and get rid of him without any danger to himself. So he found a thin hollow log and began beating upon it like a drum. Then he ran up to Wolf as fast as he could, crying out: "The soldiers are hunting for you! You heard their drum. The soldiers are after you."

Wolf was very much frightened of soldiers. "Let me go, let me go!" he shouted.

Rabbit was purposely slow in untying him and had barely freed him when Wolf broke away and ran as fast as he could into the woods. Then Rabbit returned home, laughing to himself over how he had fooled Wolf and feeling satisfied that he could have the girls to himself for a while.

Near the girls' house was a large peach orchard, and one day they asked Rabbit to shake the peaches off the tree for them. So they went to the orchard together, and he climbed up into a tree to shake the peaches off. While he was there, Wolf suddenly appeared and called out: "Rabbit, old fellow, I'm going to even the score with you. I'm not going to leave you alone until I do."

Rabbit raised his head and pretended to look at some people off in the distance. Then he shouted from the treetop: "Here is that fellow Wolf you've been hunting for!" At this, Wolf took fright and ran away again.

Sometime after this, Rabbit rested against a tree trunk that leaned toward the ground. Then, when he saw Wolf coming toward him, he stood up so the bent tree trunk pressed against his shoulder.

"I have you now," said Wolf, but Rabbit quickly replied: "Some people told me that if I held this tree up with the great power I have, they would bring me four hogs in payment. Now, I don't like hog meat as well as you do, so if you take me, they'll give the hogs to you."

Wolf's greed was excited by this, and he said he was willing to hold up the tree. So he squeezed in beside Rabbit, who said, "You must hold it tight, or it will fall." Rabbit then ran off, and Wolf stood with his back pressed hard against the bent tree-trunk until he finally decided he could stand it no longer. He jumped away quickly so the tree would not fall upon him. Then he saw only a leaning tree rooted in the earth. "That Rabbit is the biggest liar," he cried. "If I can catch him, I'll certainly fix him."

After that, Wolf hunted for Rabbit every day until he found him lying in a nice grassy place. He was about to spring upon him when Rabbit said, "My friend, I've been waiting to see you again. I have something good for you to eat. Somebody killed a pony out there in the road. If you wish, I'll help you drag it out of the road to a place where you can feast off it."

"All right," Wolf said, and he followed Rabbit out to the road where a pony was lying asleep.

"I'm not strong enough to move the pony by myself," said Rabbit, "so I'll tie its tail to yours and help you by pushing."

Rabbit tied their tails together carefully so as not to awaken the pony. Then he grabbed the pony by the ears as if he were going to lift it. Instead, the pony woke up, jumped to its feet, and ran away, dragging Wolf behind. Wolf struggled to free his tail, but he could only scratch the ground with his claws.

"Pull with all your might!!," Rabbit shouted after him.

"How can I pull with all my might," Wolf cried, "when I'm not standing on the ground?"

By and by, however, Wolf got loose, and then Rabbit had to go into hiding for a long time.

# 9

# The Creation Story

A *Salinan Story*

The earth is a great island floating in a sea of water and suspended at each of the four cardinal points by a cord hanging down from the sky vault, which is of solid rock. When the world grows old and worn out, the people will die, and the cords will break and let the earth sink into the ocean, and all will be water again. The Indians are afraid of this.

When all was water, the animals were above in Gälûñ'lätï, beyond the arch; but it was very crowded, and they wanted more room. So they wondered what was below the water, and at last, Dâyuni'sï, "Beaver's Grandchild," the little Water-beetle, offered to go and see if it could learn. It darted in every direction over the water's surface but could find no firm place to rest. Then it dived to the bottom and came up with some soft mud, which grew and spread on every side until it became the island we call the earth. It was afterward fastened to the sky with four cords, but no one remembers who did this.

At first, the earth was flat and very soft and wet. The animals were anxious to get down and sent out different birds to see if it was yet dry, but they found no place to alight and came back again to Gälûñ'lätï. Then, at last, it seemed to be time, and they sent out the Buzzard and told him to go and prepare for them. This was the Great Buzzard, the father of all the buzzards we see now. He flew all over the earth, low down near the ground, and it was still soft. When he reached the Cherokee country, he was exhausted, and his wings began to flap and strike the ground, and wherever they hit the earth, there was a valley, and where they turned up again, there was a mountain. When the animals above saw this, they were afraid that the whole world would be mountains, so they called him back, but the Cherokee country remains full of mountains to this day.

When the earth was dry and the animals came down, it was still dark, so they got the sun and set it on a track to go every day across the island from east to west, just overhead. It was too hot this way, and Tsiska'gïlï', the Red Crawfish, had his shell scorched a bright red so that his meat was spoiled; and the Cherokee did not eat it. So the conjurers put the sun another hand breadth higher in the air, but it was still too hot. So they raised it another time, and another, until it was seven handbreadths high and just under the sky arch. Then it was right, and they left it so. This is why the conjurers call the highest place Gûlkwâ'gine Di'gälûñ'lätiyûñ', "the seventh height," because it is seven hand-breadths above the earth. Every day the sun goes under this arch and returns at night on the upper side to the starting place.

There is another world under this, like ours in everything—animals, plants, and people—save that the seasons are different. The streams that come down from the mountains are the trails by which we reach this underworld, and the springs at their heads are the doorways by which we enter it, but to do, this one must fast and go to water and have one of the underground people for a guide. Moreover, we know that the seasons in the underworld are different from ours because the water in the springs is always warmer in winter and cooler in summer than in the outer air.

When the animals and plants were first made—we do not know by whom—they were told to watch and keep awake for seven nights, just as young men now fast asleep awake when they pray to their medicine. They tried to do this, and nearly all were awake through the first night, but the next night several dropped off to sleep, and third-night others were asleep, and then others, until, on the seventh night, of all the animals, only the owl, the panther, and one or two more were still awake. These were given the power to see and go about in the dark and prey on the birds and animals that must sleep at night. Of the trees, only the cedar, the pine, the spruce, the holly, and the laurel were awake to the end, and to them, it was given to be always green and to be greatest for medicine, but to the others, it was said: "Because you have not endured to the end you shall lose your, hair every winter."

Men came after the animals and plants. At first, there were only a brother and sister until he struck her with a fish and told her to multiply, and so it was. In seven days, a child was born to her, and after that, every seven days, another, and they increased very fast until there was a danger that the world could not keep them. Then it was made that a woman should have only one child in a year, and it has been so ever since.

# 10

# When Tcikabis Trapped the Sun

An Innu Legend

A long time ago, Tcikabis thought about visiting the sky; he told his sister, and she tried to talk him out of doing such a foolish thing; Tcikabis ignored his sister's advice, found the tallest tree near his village and climbed to the very top. When he looked up at the sky, the moon was far above where he was; he decided to use his magic to make the tree grow towards the sky. He hung onto a branch and leaned towards the trunk; he blew his breath on the trunk; the tree began to grow, moving towards the sky.

Tcikabis once again climbed to the top of the tree; he reached up to touch the moon, but it was still far out of his reach; once again, he took hold of a branch and blew his breath on the truck. The tree began to grow taller and faster this time; when it stopped, Tcikabis climbed to the top again. He was again disappointed; he could not reach the moon above. Finally, Tcikabis used his magic once more; this time, the tree grew taller and taller; when it stopped, he climbed to the top and stepped out onto a branch. Looking around, Tcikabis carefully stepped off the branch; his feet found the road across the moon; he walked a short way before sitting down to rest; he was exhausted and fell into a deep sleep.

A short time later, Tcikabis was woken up by a loud thunderous noise; he sat up, looked around and was blinded by a light coming toward him. Then, he suddenly heard, "Move out of the way!! ", Tcikabis replied, "No, I'm exhausted; you can go around me."

The Sun said, "If I don't follow the moon road, I will travel too close to the trees; they will catch fire, move off the road and let me pass."

Tcikabis mocked the sun, "You can jump over me; I'm not moving or getting out of the way." Very well" the sun approached and passed over Tcikabis so closely that his clothes began to catch fire; Tcikabis used his magic to protect himself but not before most of his clothes burned away, and much of his hair was singed off. Tcikabis was mad and yelled at the sun, "I'll get you back for doing this, me," the sun continued on his along the moon road unabated. Finally, Tcikabis climbed and went home; his sister saw him half-naked and burnt.

"What happened to you !!", Tcikabis said, "I was resting on the moon road, the sun came to close me and burnt me." But, unfortunately, Tcikabis didn't tell his sister the whole truth; he did not tell her that he was the author of his own misery; he said, "I'll get my revenge for what he did to me."

His sister told him not to make trouble with the sun; it may harm everyone. Tcikabis ignored his sister's advice; he began to plan his revenge; he used his magic to make a large rope net. He would climb the tree and capture the sun on the moon road. Tcikabis climbed the tree and set his trap; the sun came along the moon road and was caught in the rope net; the world suddenly went dark. His sister yelled, "Brother!! release the sun; bad things will happen to our people". The long night began, plants that needed the sun began to die, no vegetables grew, flowers didn't bloom, and the people were starving and getting angry at Tcikabis.

Tcikabis said, "If I release my rope net, my magic will not keep me safe from getting burnt to death trying to cut the apish." Tcikabis decided he should call upon the smallest animals to help him; they could hide in the shadow of the apish and chew through the apish, releasing the sun. One by one, the turtle, the rabbit and the squirrel tried to hide behind the rope and chew through the net; there all retreated when it got too hot for them to continue. Finally, a small mouse decided he would try; Tcikabis took him to the top of the tree and let him run up the rope; the mouse chewed and chewed while hiding under the rope. Suddenly, the apish broke, and the sun emerged; the world returned to the way it was in the past.

# 11

# How Deer Fawns got their Spots

*A Sioux Legend*

Many generations ago, when only animals occupied the earth, Great Spirit was reminiscing about all the four-legged creatures; he admired how they survived with his assistance. He helped the Mountain Lions and Grizzly Bear; he gave them sharp claws for protection and great strength for survival. Likewise, he gave the great Wolf sharp teeth and the Coyote quick wits to escape danger. He gave the Beaver giant teeth for chewing down trees for his lodge, a broad flat tail to signal danger and webbed feet to enable swimming swiftly underwater. Birds could escape danger by flying away with the feathers given to them; rabbits and Deer were given speed to escape those who wished to harm them.

While Great Spirit was reminiscing, mother Deer approached him with her new fawn stumbling along behind her; she said, "Great Spirit, you have been generous to all of us; you gave me the ability to leap and run to escape my enemies, others have sharp claws and sharp teeth for protection. Yet, my little one has no protection; how will she survive when those around her have such great gifts; how will my little ones survive?".

Great Spirit thought for a moment, then spoke, " Your worries as a mother have great meaning; I will help your children to survive." The great spirit called out to the little fawn to come by his side; she approached him with wobbly legs, unsure of her step. Great Spirit reached down and grabbed some plants; he crushed them in his hand; he added some soil from the forest floor and made a natural paint. Then, with his great hands, he painted spots all over the little fawn; and finally, he blew a great breath and took away any smell she gave off.

Great Spirit spoke, "Little one...when you are in danger, lay down on the ground and keep very still; no one will see you, your new spots will hide you from danger; keep still, and no other creature will find your scent except your mother".

## 12

## Beaver Meat

A Blackfoot Legend

A long time ago, there lived a father who loved to hunt and eat beaver meat. He especially enjoyed boiled tail. Over the years, his son had watched his father pursue hundreds of beaver; he told his father he should stop hunting them so much. He'd repeatedly warned his father that beavers were sacred and gave the local medicine man his magic powers to heal the sick.

His father did not listen and continued to hunt beaver with abandon; his son warned him, "The beaver will catch you and end your days." The father ignored his son's warning and went out to hunt more beaver. Then, across a nearby creek, his father spotted a beaver hole in the clay bank just above the water; he'd just spotted a beaver entering the burrow. His father crossed the creek and went headfirst into the burrow to kill the beaver with his knife; just as he entered, the beaver used his great teeth to bite into the father's shoulder, taking hold of the deer hide.

His son was not far away and heard his father yelling for help; he jumped over the bank and grabbed his father's heels; his father thought another beaver was attacking him. He cried, "I'm begging you; please let me go; I'll give you my knife." He reached back and threw his knife toward his feet, but his feet were not freed. He yelled again, "I beg of you, let me go; I will give you my hunting arrows and bow"; he threw his arrows and bow towards his feet. Not making a sound, his son released his father's feet, picked up the knife, arrows, and bow, and silently returned to the village. The beaver in the burrow released his bite and disappeared deeper into the burrow; the father slipped back out of the burrow, frightened by being alive.

His father eventually returned to the village and his tipi; he said nothing of his encounter with the beavers or the loss of his weapons. His son watched his father leave his tipi and wander towards the berry patch; he grabbed his father's knife, arrows, and bow and returned them to his father's hunting pouch.

When his father returned, he asked, "Where's your knife, arrows, and bow" his father answered, "I gave to the beaver(s) I was hunting in exchange for my life." The son said, "I told you they would catch you someday" the father never hunted beaver again.

# 13

# Origin of Language

A Sanpoils Story

During the dark winter months, many birds fly south but not all; many ducks stay close to open water and plentiful food. Many hunters try without success to hunt the wily ducks; when they hear the slightest noise, they will all take to the air at once, making a whistling sound.

One early winter morning, two hunters had some success; each managed to bring down one duck a piece; the rest flew away, making a great whistling sound. The two began to argue about the origin whistling sound; one hunter said it came from the duck bill, and the other said it came from the wings as they took to the air. The argument continued as they walked back to their village; neither one of the hunters could win the fight, so they decided they would let the Chief decide.

The two hunters entered the Chief's big house and presented their arguments about where the duck's whistling came from; the Chief looked at the two hunters, the dead ducks and said the duck couldn't make the noise he needed to hear. The Chief called upon the clan leaders to assemble and listen to the argument in their language and decide the origin of the duck's whistling noise.

The assembled clan leaders listened to the arguments and then decided it would be best to go to the hunting grounds and hear the whistling sound themselves. So the clan leaders and their people went down to the lake where the ducks could usually be found; they strolled toward the edge of the reeds, being as quiet as they could until it was time To make the ducks fly.

When the signal was given, the people behind their read suddenly stood up and began to Hoot and Holler; the ducks took to the air, their wings flapping furiously and their bills making noise. After the ducks had flown to the other side of the lake, the people assembled and again tried to determine where the noise came from; They could not agree whether the noise came from The ducks furiously flapping their wings or the noise coming from their beaks. The people could not decide, so they decided to walk around to the other side of the lake and again frightened the ducks into the air. Once assembled on the lake's far side, the people again begin to Hoot and holler, scaring the ducks into flight.

The ducks took to the air previously beating their wings and making noises from their beaks, those assembled again tried to determine where the noise was coming from, but to no avail. As the conversation continued, tempers flared, and people began to get angry; The people assembled soon divided into two groups, those who believed the noise came from the wings and those who thought the noise came from the beaks.

Over the winter months, the divided sides continued to argue and decided to move further apart; they moved to new hunting grounds, built new lodges and chose a new Leader. They developed a new language they called themselves by another name as time passed.

As the years passed, they discovered many new things in their new territories, and over time, new names were given to these new places and things. As disagreements arose within the group, the people would again split, with one group moving further away. Each time a group split away, the language changed, and they would choose a new leader. Over time the great separation and migration created many new dialects, customs new languages.

# 14

# The Woman and the White Bear

An Inuit Legend

A long time ago, in the cold and frosty north lived the people known as the Eskimo Inuit; they lived in the cold and icy arctic and fed themselves on the abundant salmon, seals, and other creatures that inhabited their territory. Most of the men in the village were hunters; they travelled far to hunt on the snow and ice and cut holes to capture the salmon from beneath the ice. A very old woman lived in the village; she was unmarried and had no children to hunt and fish for her. Many others in the village would share their food with her as it was their way of ensuring everyone had food. Though she was well looked after, her life was lonely, and she wanted a family of her own. In the evening, many villagers could see her walking along the shoreline, glancing over the snow and ice, hoping that the Creator would bring her a son.

On one very cold and windy day, while the old woman was walking along the shoreline, she saw a very tiny, sickly white

Bear curled up in the deep snow. Though she had no children of her own and her instincts as a mother took over, she walked over; I took a little white Bear into her arms and held him close. She said, "I will look after you, little one, and raise you as my son; your name will be Kunik.

The old woman carried the sickly white Bear to her home; she gathered what food she had, began feeding the white Bear, and kept him warm in her lap. Kunik started to grow and gain weight as time passed, and the old woman's love for the white Bear grew. Like many young children of the north, Kunik joined the other children of the village and would play with them all day; he would follow the other children and slide on the ice and roll about in the snow. The old woman would stand by her Igloo and smile; she was proud of her young son Kunik as he had adopted many brothers and sisters.

Like many of the village's children, Kunik grew taller, bigger and stronger over time; many of his brothers and sisters taught him how to fish; when spring was upon the village, Kunik was fishing on his own. Each morning he would leave the old woman's Igloo and return home that afternoon carrying fresh salmon for her to eat. The old woman loved her son Kunik and was very happy every time he returned home with food. She said, "My son is the best fisherman in the village; I am so proud of him!".

As two seasons passed, Kunik grew big and strong; he was by far the best hunter in the village; many of the other young hunters were very jealous of Kunik's success. The young hunters could be heard talking amongst themselves when Kunik brought home fat seals and huge salmon to his mother. The jealousy of the young hunters slowly grew into hate, they knew the older woman loved her son Kunik, but something had to be done. Finally, the young hunters decided to stop Kunik, he'd grown far too big and powerful, and they decided his life must end to protect their families.

One of Kunik's young friends happened to be nearby and heard what the young hunters were planning; he ran as quickly as possible to the older woman's Igloo to tell her what the young hunters had said. After the boy left, the old woman sat down, spoke to her son, and began to cry; She said," I will always protect you, my son, they will not kill you, and I will give my life for yours if it becomes necessary."

The village's young men were determined to end Kunik's life; they planned a great feast and believed their children were in danger. The old woman was very afraid for her son; she went home, sat down beside Kuniks and said, "You must run away and not return my son; your life is in danger here; You must hide on the ice but stay close so I can find you when I need you." Kunik was sad, he had a great love for his mother, but he knew his life was in danger and obeyed his mother's wishes; he spent his last night next to his mother before leaving quietly in the morning and disappearing onto the ice.

The young hunters were disappointed their plan had been discovered. However, their jealousy was soon overtaken by shame; they had driven one of their brothers out of the village and could see that his mother was very sad. As the days and weeks passed, many children wondered where Kunik had gone; the old woman set out onto the ice to look for her son. The old woman walked out onto the ice and called his name over and over; just when she was about to turn around, she saw something running toward her. It was Kunik; he ran up to her, reached out and gave her a great hug; she hugged back and began to cry. Kunik had grown big and strong; his white coat was clean and glistened in the sunshine; he was so happy to be reunited with his mother.

Kunik could see that his mother was hungry; he dug a great hole in the snow and asked his mother to stay out of the wind while he went and hunted for them. Kunik returned a short time later with a great fat seal; his mother was glad; she took out her knife and cut the seal into blubber pieces. They shared a meal and talked about Kunik's adventures on the ice; he'd found some other brothers and sisters out on the ice, and he was happy, but he missed home. After eating and visiting for a long time, the old woman bundled her seal meat and began to walk home; she was happy she had found her son.

Over time as the woman aged, she would go out onto the ice and visit her son, he would bring her fresh salmon and meat, and she would never go hungry again. Many of the young Hunters had now grown into men; they now truly understood that the love between a mother and her son cannot be broken. So they went to the old woman's Igloo and told her that she did not have to go onto the ice to see her son; Kunik was welcome to come home to join his brothers and sisters again.

# 15

# The Legend of White Horse Plains

An Assiniboine Love Story

Many generations ago, in the central plains of Turtle island, there was an Assiniboin Indian Chief who had a very beautiful daughter; He wanted her to be married, and two chiefs from faraway lands visited his lodge. One came from the north, Cree, and the other came from the east, Sioux. The Cree Chief offered the Assiniboin Indian Chief a prized and rare item in exchange for his daughter's hand in marriage; it was a white horse brought up from the south and was known to be as swift as the wind, strong and sturdy. It was rumoured that the white devil, as it was called, outrun any horse, outlast any horse, and sometimes go 3 or 4 days without eating food or water; this was a great gift.

The Assiniboine Indian Chief gave much thought and succumbed to the Cress Chiefs' gift of the white horse; The powerful Medicine Man of the nation favoured an alliance between their two nations. However, some people within the Assiniboine Indian Chiefs nation had long memories; they remembered what the Cree war parties had done to their people, bringing up a lot of old bitterness. One of those said that the Assiniboine Indian Chief should not disgrace his nation by mingling our blood with Cree blood. The Assiniboine Indian Chief listened, but the protests were in vain; he decided that the marriage would happen when the other Sioux chief was outside the territory.

Not long after the Assiniboine Indian Chief announced the marriage of his daughter to the Cree chief, one of his people left the village and sought out the other chief to tell him that he was not chosen as they wanted to be married to the Assiniboine Indian Chief's beautiful daughter. On the day of the marriage ceremony, The Cree Chief arrived riding a fine grey horse; behind was the gleaming white horse carrying many additional gifts for the Assiniboine Indian Chief.

The marriage ceremony took place, the gifts, including the great white horse, were given to the Assiniboine Indian Chief, and the union was complete. A great feast followed the marriage ceremony, and many other people from the Creed Sue and Assiniboine attended the wedding. Later that afternoon, one of the guests saw a cloud of dust and Riders approaching the Assiniboine Village very quickly. Indian chief saw that it was the Sioux chief who disapproved of having his daughter's hand in marriage; It appeared as though he was bringing a war party with him.

Is Assiniboine Indian chief told his daughter and her groom To ride away quickly and only come back when it was safe to do so; The groom mounted his gray horse, and his bride jumped upon the great white horse. They rode away as fast as they could with the Sioux Chief and his war party not far behind them; they rode for their lives as arrows began to fall around them. One arrow struck the gray horse, and the groom jumped onto the back of the white horse with his bride; they continued to ride as fast as they could. The Sioux Indian chief knew that his arrows were within range and told his war party to kill the bride, the groom and the great white horse. As the arrows began to fall, two arrows hit the groom, and three arrows hit the bride, causing them to fall off the great white horse dead on the ground.

The Sioux Chief in his war party continued to fire arrows at the white horse, and the Sioux Chief and his war party followed \the white horse into a nearby forest but lost sight of him. The Sioux Chief in his war party searched, but they could never find the great white horse.

The Assiniboine Indian chief retrieved the bodies of his daughter and her groom; they were buried together near the village. For many years, the great white horse could be seen running across the open plain, looking towards the Assiniboine Indian village; it seemed as though he was looking for the chief's daughter and her husband.

It is said that many years later that the great white horse can still be seen running across the Great Plain looking for its riders; A great statue was erected To honour this story, the young couple who lost their lives and the great white horse that tried to save them.

# 16

# Raven fools Crow

Unknown

The story is about Raven, who lived on the west coast of turtle island in the great forest Surrounded by mountains; He was brilliant and industrious but this particular Raven was a little bit lazy. During the summer and fall seasons, many of the other animals of the forest, like the squirrel and the crows, filled days gathering food for the Long Winter season ahead.

As summer turned to fall, the raven could be seen hopping and flying between the stumps and teasing his cousin the crow about all the work he was doing, Collecting more food than he'll ever eat and hiding it in his special places. During most winters, Raven survived very well, the snow is not deep, and he could hunt and pick low-hanging berries at his leisure; The animals of the forest I've Been Told By the great Bear to expect a lot of snow that would make it very hard to find food.

With The winter season upon them, the prediction of the great Bear came to be; Great snow storms swept through the valleys, uncovering the ground and pushing with very deep snow. Has Raven circled above? He was hungry. The snow was too deep for him to hunt Nora to find food; what would he do? Raven decided to visit the squirrel; he flew to the great tree, poked his head through the hole, and saw that the squirrel had much to eat; he had pine cones, nuts, and branches berries. Raven told the squirrel he was hungry and asked the squirrel to share his food; Squirrel said," During the spring, summer and fall, you chose not to gather food; you refused to listen to the great Bear's advice about the deep snow coming. You spent your time teasing us about all the foolish work we did gathering food," Squirrel continued," Please leave my home. I am not going to share with you," With that, Raven flew away hungry.

Raven decided he would visit the Great Bear; he knew where the great Bear slept for the winter and would see that cave. So when Raven arrived at the Bear's den, he hopped along until he found the sleeping Bear; he looked around for food but could not find any; the Great Bear had eaten all of his food and was now sleeping for the winter season.

Try this time; Raven was very hungry; many of the ground creatures were sleeping, and it was eating all their food, and the squirrel refused to give him any of his food. Many of the other birds of the forest and lakes, like the white snow geese, had flown south for warmer weather and plenty of food. Raymond thought about his cousin the crow and how he might trick him into getting Raven some food.

Raven hopped off the branch. I flew up into the sky; he could see Crow's nest below and landed near a large branch. Raven said, "Cousin crow, we must discuss your upcoming potlatch" Crow replied, "I have not thought about a potlatch, nor have

I begun to plan such an event." Raven ignored cousin Crow's answer and said, 'All the animals of the forest are talking about your potlatch; they want to hear you sing, and your songs are greatly admired. You have a beautiful voice, and you don't want to disappoint people by not singing at your Potlatch, do you? '

Cousin Crow said. "Do you like my singing?" Raven replied. "The winter is long and cold, the snow is deep, and many of us are cold; you're beautiful singing wall hours to forget how empty our stomachs are." Cousin Crow Was pleased and sent to prepare for his potlatch; he began to sing loudly and started to prepare the food. In the meantime, Raven flew to all four corners of the forest and invited all the animals to Crow's potlatch; he invited the Deer, Rabbits, Jays, Mountain goats and Mice to join the great feast.

As the animals arrived, Raven welcomed every one of them to the great feast being hosted by Crow. When all the guests were seated, Crow asked for the food to be brought out; it was a great feast indeed; Raven asked Crow to sing a song before the feast began.

While all the animals were feasting on Crow's food, Raven insisted Crow continue singing throughout the meal; each time Crow would try to eat, Raven would interrupt him and insist he keeps singing. So Crow kept singing late into the night while his guest filled their stomachs to bursting; eventually, Crow's voice began to waver, and he could sing much more than Caw!! Caw!! as he tried to sing.

When the feast ended, the animals took the rest of the food home as was the custom; Crow knew that he would not go hungry; he would be invited to all their feast during the winter season. As the cold winter winds began to blow, no feast invitations arrived for Crow. However, Raven has invited all the animal feasts. Raven had fooled Crow into believing it was his feast, but Raven had welcomed everyone without telling Crow.

Poor Crow, his singing voice was gone, he was hungry all the time, and he was not forced to spend his winter fighting for scraps left behind by a man. So today, you find Crow in parking lots fighting over leftovers and scraps, making the familiar Caw!! Caw!! Sound.

# 17

# The Pact of the First

A Sioux Story

When the world was created, First Man and First Woman struggled to stay alive and warm through the first Winter. First Dog struggled also. Deep in the Winter, First Dog gave birth to her pups. She huddled in the forest brush each night, longingly watching the fire, which kept First Man and First Woman warm.

First Winter was so cold that First Dog dared not leave her pups to search for food to fill her belly, fearing that her puppies would freeze to death in her absence. Instead, she curled around them, but the wind was bitter.

Her belly shrank with hunger, and soon she had no milk. The smallest pup perished, and First Dog felt her life draining away as she struggled to care for the remaining puppies. Finally, fearing for the fate of the others, she knew she had no choice but to approach the fire and ask First Woman and First Man to share their food and warmth.

Slowly, she crept to the fire and spoke to First Woman, who was heavy with child. I am a mother, said First Dog, and soon you will be a mother too. I want my little ones to survive, just as you will enjoy your little ones to stay. So I will ask you to make a pact. First Woman and First Man listened. I am about to die. Take my pups. You will raise them and call them Dog. They will be your guardians.

They will alert you to danger, keep you warm, guard your camp, and even lay down their life to protect your life and the lives of your children. They will be companions to you and all your generations, never leaving your side, as long as Mankind shall survive. In return, you will share your food and the warmth of your fire. You will treat my children with love and kindness and tend to them if they become ill, just as if they were born from your belly. And if they are in pain, you will take a sharp knife to their throat and end their misery. In exchange for this, you will have the loyalty of my children and all their offspring until the end of time.

First Man and First Woman agreed. First, Dog went to her nest in the brush, and with the last of her strength, she brought her pups to the fire one by one. As she did so, First Woman gave birth to First Child, wrapped her in Rabbit skins, and nestled First Child among the pups by the fireside. First, Dog lay down by the fire, licked her puppies, then walked away to die under the stars.

Before disappearing into the darkness, she turned and spoke again to First Man, "My children will honour this pact for all generations. But if Man breaks this pact, if you or your children's children deny even one dog food, warmth, a kind word or a merciful end, your generations will be plagued with war, hunger and disease, and so this shall remain until the pact is honoured again by all Mankind." First, Dog entered the night and returned in spirit to the creator.

# 18

# The Story of Jumping Mouse

The Sundance Story of the Prairies

One time there was a mouse who lived with other mice, and this little Mouse kept hearing a roaring in his ears. He couldn't figure out what it was. So all the time, everywhere he went, as he went about his Mouse's business, his little whiskers going, looking into nooks and crannies, gathering things, taking seeds from one place to another, he kept hearing this roaring, and he wondered what it was.

Sometimes he would ask the other mice, "I hear this roaring in my ears; what is it?" And the other mice always said, "We don't hear anything. So you must be crazy; get back to work. Accumulate!" So he got back to work, being a mouse, and did all the things that mice do, but he couldn't get the roaring out of his ears, and finally, he resolved that he would try to find out what it was.

Very timidly, he went to the edge of where the mice lived around the roots of trees and bushes. As soon as he got outside where the mice lived, he saw a raccoon. The raccoon said, "Hello, little brother," and he looked up and said, "Hello, brother." And he said, "You know, I hear this roaring in my ears all the time, and I wonder what it is." So the raccoon spoke, "Oh, that's easy. I know what that is, that's the great river, and I go there every day to wash my food."

Little Mouse was excited because this was the first time that anyone had ever said that what he heard was real, and so he started scheming in his Mouse's way about how he would take the proof back to all the other mice and then they wouldn't think he was strange anymore. So the raccoon said, "Yes, I'll take you to the river," and little Mouse followed him.

Finally, they got to the edge of the great river, to a little eddy on the great river, but little Mouse had never seen anything like that before in his life, this fantastic expanse of water. Where mice live, the only water they see is rainwater and dew. They don't see big bodies of water; too little Mouse was just immense, and he timidly went up to the edge of the water. He looked in and freaked because he saw a mouse in there! He jumped back, but nothing happened, and he looked again and saw a mouse in there. He'd seen his reflection for the first time.

The raccoon led him down to the bank of the river, and at one place, he put his hand in and tasted the water. finally, the raccoon said, "I have to go about my business and find food and wash it in the river, but I'll take you to a friend of mine." So the raccoon took little Mouse to his brother, Frog.

A giant green frog was sitting on the river's edge, half in and half out. Little Mouse said to him, "Hello, brother," and the Frog replied, "Hello, brother." And they talked for a while, and the Frog told him about his life, about how he had been given the gift to live half in the water and half out of it. He was all green on top and white underneath. He told little Mouse, "When Thunderbird flies, you will always find me here, but when winter-man comes, I will be gone."

That sounded pretty good to little Mouse, and the Frog said, "Do you want medicine?" Little Mouse said, "Sure, I'd like medicine, yes." And then the Frog said, "O. K., just crouch as low as you can get and jump up as high as you can jump."

So little Mouse did that. First, he got down as low as he could, and then he jumped up as high as a mouse. And when he jumped up, he saw the sacred mountains and then fell back down and into the water.

Nothing like this had ever happened to him before, and he scurried out of the water and was furious. He said, "You tricked me; that's no medicine; I fell in the water." And the Frog said, "Yes, you fell in the water. You're wet. But you're safe; you're alive, aren't you?" And little Mouse said, "Yes, I am." And the Frog said to him, "What did you see when you jumped up?" Little Mouse said, "Oh, yes, yes. I saw the sacred mountains." And the Frog said to him, "You have a new name. Your name is Jumping Mouse."

Jumping Mouse thanks the Frog for having taught him, and then he says, "It's time to go back to my people. I want to tell them about the sacred mountains." He has changed. Instead of saying, "I want to prove to those bastards that the river exists," he is excited. He's seen the sacred mountains and wants to go back and share his vision with his people. He speaks in innocence because he has learned from the Frog. He wants to go back to innocence to tell them about it, and in innocence, he will be able to return. The Frog tells him, "It's easy to return to your people. Just keep the sound of the river behind you. The roaring that you heard is now your medicine. You know what it is, and you can return to your people."

Mice cannot go in a straight line because they can see close, but with the medicine behind him, Jumping Mouse can return. He has always heard it, but now he can navigate by it; he has a direction.

Jumping Mouse keeps the medicine behind him and returns to where the other mice live. He says to them, "You know that roaring in my ears? The great river and raccoon took me there, and I met a frog. The Frog gave me medicine, and I jumped up and saw the sacred mountains." But they looked at him strangely because he was all wet. He had forgotten about falling into the river, but they started whispering. They said, "An animal must have had him in its mouth. There must be something wrong with him. There must be some terrible pollution that he was in the jaws of death and wasn't taken. Very dangerous person." They didn't even hear what he said about the sacred mountains.

Poor Jumping Mouse was just crestfallen at this because he had wanted to tell them about what he had seen so they could see it too, but they couldn't. You cannot see through the eyes of another without giving him your eyes, and they could not do that. So he stayed with them for a while because they were his people, but finally, he resolved to go on and find the sacred mountains.

He told them about his resolve, and they said, "You're insane; you can't do it; the spots will get you." They knew, all mice know, that out on the prairie, eagles can swoop down and get mice. But mice do not know eagles. They are too distant from them, and so they only see them as spots in the sky. They can see close into the little things of the earth, but when they look up and far away, they only see spots. And this is a paradox, but eagles, when they are close to the ground only see things as a blur. The mice's fear of spots is real because eagles are real and get mice, and Jumping Mouse is terrified but goes on. Out onto the prairie, he went, his whiskers feeling, dodging this way and that, feeling the spots pressing down on his back. The prairie is where the great animals meet and travel far; it is a strange place for a mouse. Jumping Mouse went into it with fear, and finally, he came to a circle of sweet sage.

The circle of sage was a haven, a cover from the spots, and sweet sage is a plant that you cannot eat but which is used by the Indians for incense, prayer, something healing and beautiful. There in the sweet sage was an old, old mouse. Long braids, an old mouse. Jumping Mouse was joyous to meet someone of his kind he could talk to out in this strange place. The clump of sage was a haven and a paradise for mice. There were seeds and roots to crawl into and everything a mouse could want there.

He went up to the old Mouse and said, "Grandfather, I heard a roaring in my ears, and I have been to the great river." The old Mouse said, "Yes, I too heard the roaring, and I too have been to the great river." Jumping Mouse was excited because, for the first time, he had found a mouse who had shared his experience. So they talked about the river and the everyday things they knew. Jumping Mouse was increasingly excited, and he said, "And then I met the frog, and he told me to jump up, and I jumped up, and I saw the sacred mountains." The old Mouse was silent for a long time and said, "My grandson, the great river is real, and we have both been there and tasted its water, but the sacred mountains are just a myth. They don't exist." Jumping Mouse was crushed and disappointed by this, and the old Mouse said, "Stay with me and grow old with me here. This is a perfect place for mice, and we have both been further than any other mouse."

Jumping Mouse resolves to go on, and the old Mouse is upset.

He says, "You can't do that; the spots will get you." But Jumping Mouse is resolved, and he leaves the old Mouse in the sage. He goes out onto the prairie, and he is terrified. He can feel the spots, feel them pressing in. He knows they are there every moment; his little whiskers are going fast, and finally, he gets out to the prairie and comes to a stand of chokecherry bushes. Chokecherries are good to eat, but they make you fantastically thirsty. The more you eat, the more thirst you have.

Jumping Mouse is out of breath and thankful for a haven and cover from the spots, and as he lies there panting, he hears a great sighing slowly, up and down. And he looks up and sees that it is a great animal. So jumping Mouse thinks, "I am so small, and this great being is so large," and he forgets his fear in his awe and goes up to the animal and says, "Hello, great brother," and it replies, "Hello, little brother," and Jumping Mouse asks, "Who are you?" and he says, "I am a Buffalo, and I am dying." When he hears this, little Mouse is overcome with sadness that this great being he has just met is dying, and he says to him, "What can I do to make you well? Is there any medicine that will make you well?" And the Buffalo says, "I have talked with my medicine, and it has told me that there is only one thing that will make me well, and that is the eye of a mouse, and there is no such thing as a mouse."

This just freaked Jumping Mouse, and he ran back, his little whiskers going, his tail behind him until he reached some cover. But from a safe place, he heard the breathing again, getting slower and slower, and he felt tremendous compassion for the Buffalo. "I am so small," he thought, "and the buffalo is great and beautiful." So, finally, he came out from his hole, taking two steps forward and one step back, his tail dragging but resolved to speak to his great brother. "I want to tell you something," he said, "there is such a thing as a mouse, and I am a mouse."

"Thank you very much, little brother," the Buffalo replied. "I will die happy knowing there is such a thing as a mouse. But it is too much to ask you to give one of your eyes." But Jumping Mouse told him, "No, I am so small, and you are so great that I would like to give you one of my eyes and make you well." And immediately as he said that, one of his eyes flew out of his head, and the Buffalo jumped up, strong, his hooves pounding on the earth and his great head dancing and hooking. He was strong and said, "I know who you are. You are Jumping Mouse, and you have been to the river, jumped up, and seen the sacred mountains. You are on your way to them. I can guide you across the prairie, for I am one of the great beings of the prairie. Run underneath me. I know you are afraid of the spots, and I will protect you from them. So you will be safe, and I will take you across the prairie to the edge of the sacred mountains. But I can't take you farther than that because I am a creature of the prairie, and I must stay here to give away to the people. It will be too steep if I go up onto the sacred mountains, and I will fall and crush you."

So Jumping Mouse runs underneath the Buffalo across the prairie, his hooves just pounding, dust flying, shaking the earth and little Mouse is frightened at the great power of the Buffalo. He knows he is safe, but this is worse, trying to keep up with a goddamn buffalo! Finally, they get to the prairie's edge, and he is exhausted. He comes creeping out from underneath the great Buffalo, thankful to be alive. He looks up at the great gift and says, "That was something!" And the Buffalo says, "You didn't need to worry, little brother. I am a buffalo, and I know where I place every footstep. I am a great dancer and light on my feet. I could see you underneath me, and you were perfectly safe."

So the Buffalo left Jumping Mouse at the edge of the sacred mountains, and he looked around. Who should he see now but a wolf, sitting there - a big beautiful wolf, just sitting on his haunches, looking around one place or another? And he goes up to him and says, "Hello, brother Wolf." And the wolf says, "Wolf, wolf, yes, I'm a wolf, wolf, yes, wolf," and then he sort of sits back, and a beatific grin comes across his, and he doesn't say any more. His mind wanders and slips away. And Jumping Mouse can't figure that out. What the hell's going on? So he comes up again, saying, "Hello, brother wolf," and the wolf says, "Wolf, wolf, yes wolf, wolf, yes, I'm a wolf, yes," and his voice trails off as his mind slips again.

So Jumping Mouse wonders what is going on, and he goes a little distance away and listens to the beating of his heart; the sound of his heart is beating like a drum inside him. And he remembered all the things that had happened to him. He recalled that when the Buffalo was dying, the thing that would make him well was a mouse's eye, and he figured that was good medicine. "I've got good medicine, a lot of power in the eye of a mouse." And he resolves that he will give his other eye to the wolf, which will make him well. So he goes up to the wolf, and he says, "Brother wolf," and the wolf begins to speak, "Wolf, wolf," but Jumping Mouse stops him and says, "I want to give you one of my eyes," and immediately his eye, his last eye, is gone and he's blind, and the wolf jumps up and says, Yes, I'm a wolf. I know who you are.

You are Jumping Mouse. You have been to the great river, the Frog has shown you the sacred mountains, the Buffalo has brought you to me, and I can guide you to the medicine lake at the top of the holy mountains."

Little Mouse is blind now, and all he has is his whiskers. He can touch but has given up all his old ways of seeing. He can only handle things close now. The wolf takes him up from the prairie, through the pines, and "stands in place," Finally, they get to the open country at the top of the mountain. There are no trees there, no cover, nothing for a mouse. They get to the edge of the medicine lake, and the wolf tells him, "We are here. We are at the medicine lake." And he sits Jumping Mouse down by it.

Jumping Mouse takes his hand, puts it in the water, and tastes it, and it's good; it's beautiful. And then, the wolf describes what he can see in the medicine lake. He says, "In medicine, lakes are reflected all the people's lodges. The whole world is reflected there. The medicine lake is the reflection. It is a symbol of reflection. They sit there, and Jumping Mouse knows it is time for the wolf to go about business and travel to other parts of the world. It is time for the Eagles to get him.

It is an open place, and the eagles will see him and come as soon as his guide is gone. He is blind, and he can't see them. The wolf feels tremendous compassion and feeling for Jumping Mouse, his brother, and his heart stretches out to him, and the wolf cries. Then he leaves, and Jumping Mouse is left alone, blind, nothing but looking within, and he can feel the spots on his back, just pressing in hard. And then he hears the rush of wind and wings, and then there is a great shock, and everything is black.

The next thing he knows, he can see colours. He can see! He can see colours. And he's amazed, astonished; he doesn't know if he's dreaming or what is happening. But he's alive, and he can see colours. Then he sees a blur of colours moving toward him, something green and white moving his way, and from the colours comes a voice. "You want medicine?" And

Jumping Mouse says, "Yes, I'd like medicine." And the voice says, "Just get down as far as you can and jump up as high as you can." So little Mouse gets down as low as he can and jumps up as high as he can jump, and when he does, the wind catches him and swirls him up and up and up in the air. And the voice calls out from below him, "Grab hold of the wind!" So little Mouse reaches out and grabs hold of the wind as hard as he can, and the wind takes him higher and higher until everything gets clearer. Crystal clear, and he can see all the great beings of the prairie, the Buffalo, the wolf on the mountain, and he looks down into the medicine lake, and there are all the lodges of the people reflected, and on the edge of the medicine lake, he sees his friend the Frog. So he calls down to him, "Hello, brother Frog," and the Frog calls back to him, "Hello, brother Eagle."

*Reprinted with Ojibwe translations by Richard Nanawin*

# 19

# How Music came to the World

An Aztec Story

Two powerful gods within the Aztec pantheon sometimes fought and sometimes didn't. As it happened, they met on a very windy, high plain one day. This would stand to reason, as one of them was Tezcatlipoca, the sky god, and the other was Quetzalcoatl, the god of the Wind.

Tezcatlipoca spoke first to Quetzalcoatl by snidely asking. "What took you so long?"

Quetzalcoatl answered over his shoulder. "I've been busy with this hurricane season whipping up the waves."

They argued for a while over the importance of wave whipping in their meeting. Then, finally, Tezcatlipoca yelled out to his companion. "You stop huffing for a moment and listen. What do you hear?"

"Nothing. So?"

"Yeah. See?" Responded Quetzalcoatl. "Exactly my point. Without all the noises you make with the Wind, the waves, the other noises of small creatures, and that of the occasional volcano tossing up new earth and rock, there is nothing. I mean exactly nothing! No one sings. No one plays a note. So we need to wake up the world, Wind. And I don't mean hurricanes. We need music!"

"Music?" said Quetzalcoatl. I don't even know what that word is."

"I know," the sky god said. "But, I'll tell you who does: the Sun. He surrounds himself with singers and music-makers who play and sing for him all day long, and that so-and-so won't share their music with us, which is evident because you don't even know what it is."

"He won't share?" said Quetzalcoatl. "That's not fair!"

"I know," said Tezcatlipoca. "And that's why I want you to go to the House of the Sun and bring the best singers and musicians. Remember," he said as the wind god unfolded his wings. "We need to wake up the world. We need music!"

With one mighty flap, Quetzalcoatl hurled himself into the air. He flew over land and sea, searching the endless coastline for a single beach. He knew only one way he could travel to the House of the Sun.

After finding it, he landed and called out the names of the sky god's three servants: Cane and Conch, Water Woman and Water Monster. When they all stood before him, he ordered them to build a bridge.

They grabbed hold of each other and began to grow tall and thin, and twine together like twine makes a rope. Finally, they turned into a strong rope bridge that disappeared into the sky.

Quetzalcoatl climbed the bridge, following it higher and higher as the earth grew smaller and smaller below.

Finally, he came to the House of the Sun realm, and he could see the palace towers shimmering in the distance. However, he also discovered that getting to them was not as easy as arriving in the Sun's realm. He had to grope around to find his way through a maze of streets with high walls. He kept getting lost and going around in circles.

Nearly ready to give up, he heard a beautiful sound he had never heard before. It was fantastic and bright. It was sweet and light. It was music.

Quetzalcoatl followed the sound until it led him out of the building maze. Then he saw the musicians in the great courtyard of the Sun.

The flute players were dressed in golden yellow. The wandering minstrels wore blue. The lullaby singers were dressed in white, and the singers of love songs wore red.

Suddenly the Sun saw Quetzalcoatl.

"Stop playing!" he cried. "Stop it, I say. "Stop your singing right now! It's that foul-tempered Wind! Don't even speak to him, or he will take you back to that silent planet of his!"

Quetzalcoatl lifted his wings and called to the musicians to come with him!

None of them said a word.

Again the wind god cried out, "Singers! Musicians! The Lord of the Sky commands you!" And again, the musicians remained silent.

Quetzalcoatl did not like to be ignored. He exploded with anger, like a hundred hurricanes going off at once. Lightning cracked, thunder boomed, and clouds swirled around the House of the Sun, turning the daylight into darkness. The wind god then roared as if his voice had no end. Everything fell. The Sun flickered like a tiny flame. The musicians all ran to the Wind and huddled in his arms, trembling with fear.

Instantly the Wind's anger passed. His thunder faded, and the clouds vanished. Quetzalcoatl took the musicians in his arms and left the House of the Sun, moving through the maze as if it were not even there because he was filled with great happiness as he followed the sky bridge back to earth.

The earth could also feel that something new was coming - something it needed and had secretly wished for. As the wind god came nearer, the world let out a slow sigh of relief as its fruit plants began to ripen and its flowers began to bloom with new, deeper colours. The whole planet seemed to be waking up from a long sleep.

Finally, Quetzalcoatl touched down on the earth with the musicians and singers. They looked around curiously at the silent, waiting planet. Then they began to play and started to wander as they played through forests and valleys and deserts and oceans they travelled, filling the air with music.

Soon people learned to sing and play, and so did the trees and birds, the whales and wolves, the running streams, the crickets and frogs, and every other creature.

From dawn to dusk, the melodies spread until music covered the earth.

The wind god was pleased. So was the sky god. The musicians were happy with their new home.

And ever since that day, the earth has been filled with music.

*Reprinted with Ojibwe translations by Richard Nanawin*

# 20

# The Bully and the Buffalo

A Great Plains Story

Many years ago, a. grizzly Bear wandered through the hills nearby a great river. While walking along the river bank, he saw a Buffalo standing on the trail. Buffalo did not look well, his head was hanging down, and he looked as though he was weak and very sick. "Yo! Crooked horns," said the Bear," Many have said that you are willing to go to war with me! So put on your war paint, and we will fight!."

Buffalo said, "I do not want to fight with you, Bear. "Buffalo said, "I do not want to fight; I want peace." "Yo!" said Bear, "You are a great beast with crooked horns and a coward! You want to run away like an old woman; you were terrified of me!" Bear moved closer to the Buffalo; he pulled on his long hair and pushed his nose into the dirt. Then, he yanked on Buffalo's tail and hit him in the face as hard as possible.

Buffalo said, "Bear, you have caused me much pain" Buffalo

walked away in pain and said, "I have done nothing to anger you, and you still hurt me; this was not right." Bear said, "Buffalo with crooked horns, you have the heart of an old woman; you will always fear me." Bear turned around and continued on his wanderings. While walking away, Bear turned around one more time and said," You are indeed a coward, and I will tell everyone so." Buffalo watched the Bear walk away from him. He said, "I should fight him; he was just a mean bully."

Bear, a magical beast with powers, knew precisely what Buffalo was thinking. So he came back towards Buffalo and said," What did you say about me, crooked horns?" Buffalo said, "I said nothing about you." Bear replied, "You speak with two tongues; you were thinking and talking about me in your mind; I know what you said!" So bear ran towards the Buffalo again; he mauled at him, pulled his long hair and slapped him many times. Bear then continued on his way, laughing to himself.

Buffalo stood for a moment and thought, "I should fight him; he was always picking on others and wanting the fight.". As the Bear was walking away, he again heard what Buffalo was thinking; he came back and beat him again; this happened four times. Finally, on the fifth time, Bear turned around and came running at Buffalo. Buffalo backed away, put his head down, and began pawing at earth, telling the Bear not to hurt him anymore.

Bear said, "Don't run away, you fearful old woman. Don't run away!! Stand and fight me, you coward! As Bear approached Buffalo, he kept backing away. Finally, when he was at the edge of the steep bank, he rushed forward and knocked Bear flat on his back. Buffalo stood over the Bear and pressed his great sharp black horns into the Bear's chest. "Buffalo!, cried Bear, "Spare me with your sharp horns; you will cause me great pain."

Buffalo said, "You so badly wanted to go to war; now you don't want to stand up and fight; why don't you want to fight me now!?"

As Bear scrambled to get away from Buffalo, he neared the high bank; he fell over the edge and rolled and rolled to the bottom of the river valley. From where he lay, there was crying and begging for Buffalo to help him get back up on the plateau.

Buffalo stood on the edge of the high bank; he said, "You are the very kind of person that wants to fight the weak all the time; I should come down and finish this fight and make you pay dearly for the pain you have caused others. I should leave you down there so you can't come back up and bother others." Bear cried loudly," If you help me back onto the plateau, I will make peace with everyone and fight no more."

So, at last, Buffalo let the Bear come back up on the plateau, and since then, Bear and Buffalo have been at peace, but Bear still has his bad temper.

# About the Author

Richard is Anishinaabe Aadizookaan (A traditional storyteller). He has shared stories of Nanabush and his adventures with countless children and adults on Turtle Island.

Richard Nanawin was born in 1965, a Traditional Ojibwe/Cree Storyteller from Poplar River First Nation in northern Manitoba. His Ookomisan (grandmother-grandmother) is Ojibwa/Cree from Poplar River First Nation, Manitoba. His Omishoomisan (grandfathers-grandmother) is Chippewa from Fond Du Lac Indian Nation, Michigan, USA.

*Richard Nanawin*

www.ingramcontent.com/pod-product-compliance
Lightning Source LLC
Chambersburg PA
CBHW070320120526
44590CB00017B/2757